Miniature toys

James Dunbar

This book is all about miniature toys. These miniature toys are small models of things which are bigger in real life.

You do not have to read this book from beginning to end. Just turn to the pages that interest you.

Contents

What is a miniature?

A miniature is something very small.

A miniature is a tiny model of something
which is bigger in real life.

 You can see how small this house is.

You can see by the size of the hen's egg that these are miniature toys.

Pocket toys

Some toys are made to be put in your pocket or just carried around with you.

Pocket toys are usually made of plastic or metal.

Sometimes they are found in crackers,
breakfast cereals or in large sweets.

Miniature people

There are many different types and sizes of miniature people.

Miniature people can wear all sorts of different clothes.

Some are soldiers, spacemen or even babies.

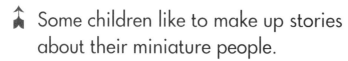 Some children like to make up stories about their miniature people.

There are lots of miniature things which go with the miniature people.

Miniature animals

There are many kinds of miniature toy animals. You can get circus, zoo and farmyard animals.

You can also get animals for a Noah's Ark.

Noah's Ark and its miniature animals has been a popular toy for over two hundred years.

Miniature houses

**A Doll's House is a
home in miniature.**

A Doll's House can show us a lot
about the way people lived
in the past.

Sometimes a Doll's House is
an exact miniature of the house
the child lived in.

Miniature shops and garages

There are miniature shops and garages and other buildings.

⬆ A miniature butcher's shop about one hundred years old.

The models look very real because they have been carefully copied from real life.

↑ A miniature toy garage made about 40 years ago.

Model villages

Some model villages are big enough to walk round.

This model village is in a town called Bourton on the Water.

The houses are made of stone.
The plants are growing and there
is a bridge over a real stream.

There is a model town in Denmark
made from over thirty five million
Lego bricks.

Glossary of words used in this book

Cracker   A cracker is a tube made of cardboard.
It often has a small present inside.

Exact miniature   An exact miniature is a tiny copy of a real thing.
It is much smaller than the real thing.

Garage   A garage is a building where cars can be kept.
It is also a place to take the car to be mended.

Metal   Metal is a hard material. Iron, gold and tin are metals.

Noah's ark   An ark is a wooden ship. Noah made an ark to save his family, himself and two of every living creature from a great flood.

Plastic   Plastic is strong and light material.
Plastic toys can be made in many different shapes.